T0109596

SEARCHING FOR GOLD IN THE KLONDIKE

A HISTORY-SEEKING ADVENTURE

by Eric Braun

CAPSTONE PRESS
a capstone imprint

Published by Capstone Press, an imprint of Capstone
1710 Roe Crest Drive, North Mankato, Minnesota 56003
capstonepub.com

Library of Congress Cataloging-in-Publication Data is available
on the Library of Congress website.
ISBN: 9781669069379 (hardcover)
ISBN: 9781669069348 (paperback)
ISBN: 9781669069355 (ebook PDF)

Summary: YOU are living through a deep recession. Unemployment is high.
There is a shortage of gold. Banks are running out of money. And then one
day, you read that prospectors have discovered gold along the Klondike River
in northern Canada. Will you venture north by boat, facing the perils of the
water along the way? Or will you take your chances on land? Step back in time
to face the dangers and decisions real people had to make as they tried to strike
it rich in the Klondike.

Editorial Credits
Editor: Alison Deering; Designer: Bobbie Nuytten; Media Researcher: Jo Miller;
Production Specialist: Whitney Schaefer

Image Credits
Alamy: Archive PL, 18, Historic Images, 75, UtCon Collection, 79; Getty Images:
Archive Photos, 42, 45, 54, 61, Bettmann, 25, clu, 58, Hulton Archive, Cover,
ilbusca, 38, 57, 81, 96, 109; Shutterstock: Jamesboy Nuchaikong, 90, optimarc, 32,
Pereslavtseva Katerina, 64, Trina Barnes, 83; Superstock: Devaney-SuperStock/
Devaney Collection, 4, Mary Evans Picture Library, 103; Wikimedia: Seattle
Public Library, 14

Printed and bound in China. PO 5827

TABLE OF CONTENTS

ABOUT YOUR ADVENTURE

YOU are living through a deep recession. Across America, unemployment is high. There is a shortage of gold. Paper money, which is tied to gold for its value, is rapidly becoming less valuable. Some banks are running out of money and closing their doors, leaving customers with nothing.

But then news comes—gold has been discovered in the Klondike. Do you dare to journey north in the hopes of striking it rich? To do so, you must choose which path to read. Chapter One sets the scene. Follow the directions at the bottom of the page as you read the stories. After you finish one path, go back and read the others for new perspectives and more adventures.

Turn the page to begin your adventure.

CHAPTER 1

DEPRESSION AND HOPE

It is 1897, and all over the United States, people feel nervous and uncertain due to the deep recession gripping the country. But then one day a story in the paper catches your eye. Ships from the Yukon—the northernmost part of Canada—have been arriving in San Francisco and Seattle. And they have been loaded down with gold.

At first, it seems too good to be true. But as you follow the story over the coming days and weeks, the news is confirmed. Prospectors have discovered gold along the Klondike River in the Yukon—and they say there is more where that came from.

Turn the page.

You begin to daydream about striking it rich. Could you really do it? The Yukon is so far away and so hard to reach. The dangers are many— grizzly bears, avalanches, starvation, shipwrecks. Temperatures in the winter can be deathly cold. And with so much money at stake, you can't ignore the possibility of another risk if you *do* strike it rich: murder.

Still, many are making the journey. People from all over the world—mostly the United States—are packing up gear and heading into the unknown. Visions of gold spur them along. Some of them are experienced prospectors, but most are not. They are regular people. Shop workers, restaurant servers, police officers, and dock hands. Fathers, husbands, and brothers. Soon, there are so many people trying to get to the Klondike that it's being called a stampede. And there is reason to hurry. Those who get there early enough can stake a legal claim to search for gold on a certain patch of land. Before long, all the gold-rich land will be claimed.

There are three main ways to get to the Yukon. Some of the stampeders take the all-water route. They sail to Alaska, then up the Yukon River to the Klondike River. That's the easiest route, but it's expensive.

Others sail to the Gulf of Alaska. They try their luck hiking over the towering glaciers near the towns of Yakutat and Valdez.

Perhaps the most common way to get there is to simply hike over the mountains. This is the least expensive, but it can take more than a year.

Soon, you've made up your mind. You'll try your luck in the Klondike. You intend to get rich.

- To be a sawmill worker outside of San Francisco, turn to page 11.

- To be a politician in Seattle, turn to page 41.

- To be a New York business owner, turn to page 71.

CHAPTER 2

SAWMILL WORKER

You've been working in the sawmill for years. It's physical and sometimes dangerous work, but you don't mind it. In fact, you feel lucky to have a job when so many people in the country are out of work.

But you do worry. The sawmill owner has been losing money in the recession, and he recently fired several workers. Some of those men were your friends. If things don't get better soon, you figure your job is on the line too.

You decide to risk it. You've saved up a decent nest egg. That—along with your last paycheck—

Turn the page.

should be enough to get you to the Klondike. Coming home will be another story, but if you find gold it will be easy enough. You'll be sailing home in style.

So, at the end of your shift one day, you tell your foreman that you quit. "If you ever see me again, I'll be stinking rich," you say.

The first thing you do is buy a train ticket to Vancouver, British Columbia. You arrive in the city with nothing but a satchel filled with clothes and a few personal items. From there, you buy a ticket on a ship and sail to Skagway, a small port town just north of Juneau, Alaska.

You step off the ship with your satchel onto a street bustling with pedestrians. You find your way to an outfitter and buy a tent, a hatchet, prospecting pans, boots and other warm clothing, plus a pistol and a rifle.

As you're paying for your gear, the outfitter asks about your trip. You tell him you plan to hike over the White Pass Trail.

"You've heard about the food law, right?" he asks. "Everyone who goes up the pass has to pack a year's worth of food."

You had not planned on carrying that much food—you'd intended to hunt for much of what you needed to eat. Carrying that much food will slow you way down. But you understand the reason for the law. Many have already starved to death on this route.

Reluctantly, you purchase flour, dried beans, cured meat, sugar, and a few other items—enough to last for a year. When you're done shopping, you only have a small amount of money left.

Though the sun is still shining, it's late, and you're tired. You rent a room in a boarding

Turn the page.

house for one final night of comfortable indoor sleep before you begin your journey.

Morning dawns, and you're about to head out for the White Pass Trail when you see someone selling horses at a livery stable. You look at all the gear you have to carry, bundled in several huge packs.

Prosepectors and packhorses set out on the White Pass Trail.

If you walk, you'll have to carry it in stages. You'll haul one load up a few miles, hide it, then return for another load—over and over. In talking to other prospectors, you know it will take at least 90 days to get over the pass using this method, and winter will be here soon enough. It will get cold and dangerous.

If you buy a horse, you could move faster. You wouldn't have to go in stages. But there are downsides of a horse—besides the cost. The White Pass Trail is narrow and riddled with boulders and sharp rocks. It's notoriously difficult for horses, and many have died making this trip.

- To go on foot, turn to page 16.
- To buy a horse, turn to page 18.

You always knew it was going to be a long, hard journey. You are prepared to take the pass on foot, and that's what you decide to do. If you spend money on a horse and it dies, that would be a devastating loss.

You hide several packs in a stand of trees along the trail and set out with two big packs. There are dozens of other stampeders on the path with you as you trudge up the mountain. A few men are chatting, but most keep their heads down, focusing on their footing as they make their way.

You begin to sweat right away, and soon you feel mosquitoes on your face and neck. Not just a couple, but dozens. You slap at the bugs and notice some of the men are doing the same. Others simply let the bugs bite them. After a few hours, you stash your packs and head down the mountain to get your next load.

After five days of slowly making your way, you are covered in mosquito bites, and you're exhausted. You pause to rest under a tree when a man with a thick black beard approaches you.

"Howdy," he says, squinting in the sun. "Name's Phillips."

You see he's not carrying any gear and know right away what he's going to ask you. Some men along the route are selling their services. They'll help carry your things—for a fee. And that fee is very high, because they know people are desperate and will pay it.

Sure enough, that's exactly what Phillips offers. "Not only easier with help, but lots of men appreciate the company," he adds, smiling.

Do you want to spend some of your last dollars on help? Can you trust this man?

- To hire Phillips, turn to page 20.
- To keep going alone, turn to page 22.

You know that winter will come soon enough, and you don't want to get caught on the pass when it does. So you decide to buy a horse.

You name her Candy and load her up with all your packs. It's a lot, but Candy is strong, and when you start passing other prospectors walking up the trail, you feel confident you made the right decision.

A prospector makes his way up the White Pass Trail.

You make good time, but on the fifth day you come to a narrow, harsh-looking part of the pass. It's been a tough climb to this point, and Candy is huffing and moving slowly. The sun is a fiery menace, and both you and Candy could use a day or two of rest.

But when you glance back at the prospectors hiking up after you, you're reminded that every day counts. Every day you're not prospecting at the Klondike is another day that someone else might find gold that could've been yours.

- To pitch camp by the creek and rest for a couple days, turn to page 24.
- To push forward, turn to page 26.

"How much?" you ask.

Phillips gives you his price, and you agree. With his help, you're able to haul all your gear at once, without going in stages. And Phillips was right—he is good company. He has colorful stories about the boomtowns that have popped up along the way to the Klondike. He has seen a few men find gold, but he's seen a lot more go home broke. He's seen men get robbed, left behind in the snow, even murdered.

You reach the Yukon River in less than a month and pay Phillips for his work. Then you get to work setting up camp on the shore of Lake Bennett and begin preparing for the final leg of your journey.

You need to build a boat to get you up the Yukon to the Klondike River, so you use your hatchet to cut down trees and prepare the wood. Thanks to your previous job in a sawmill, this is natural work for you. You hunt a moose, skin it, and use the skin to waterproof your boat. You salt and smoke the meat and pack it away for the winter.

The night before you're ready to set off on the boat, you hear a noise outside your tent. You grab your pistol and peek out. A figure is standing by your boat. It appears the man is taking something out of it.

The man turns for a second. In the light of the moon, you see that it's Phillips. You remember his stories of men being robbed and murdered out here.

• To shoot him while he isn't looking, turn to page 28.
• To confront him, turn to page 30.

You don't know if you can trust Phillips. And you can't spare the money to pay him. It will make your journey longer and harder, but you decide to go it alone. That was your original plan anyway. Why change now?

You set off on the trail. Your muscles ache every night as you lay in your tent. Your face is covered in mosquito bites. On one hand it's miserable, but on the other, it feels good to work hard for your goal.

You hike for days, which turn into weeks. After a month, you're about halfway up the path. One evening, as you're sitting by your campfire, you sense movement in the woods.

Quietly, you pick up your rifle. As you watch, a caribou steps near. You waste no time—you shoot it, skin it, and begin to cure the meat that night. This is a nice stroke of luck. You got a lot of meat and didn't have to spend time hunting.

But you make one crucial mistake. You clean the caribou close to your campsite, and that night a grizzly bear follows the smell into your camp. It is eating your meat when you surprise it.

You bang two pots together, trying to scare the bear away, but when it turns to you, it does not look scared at all. A low, menacing growl gurgles from its bloody mouth, and then suddenly it charges you. You don't even have a chance to get a shot off before it's on you, ending your search for gold in a brutal attack.

THE END

To follow another path, turn to page 9.
To learn more about the Klondike Gold Rush,
turn to page 101.

Candy has been working hard. She'll need all her strength to handle the narrow, rocky passage up ahead. You decide to camp for a couple of nights. You bathe in the creek and give Candy an extra meal as she rests in the shade.

It must have been the right decision because when you set off again, Candy is stronger than ever. You feel better too.

In a few weeks, you arrive at a small boomtown on the Yukon. You sell Candy to a fellow prospector. He's heading back down the trail to register his claim. With the money, you're able to book passage on a large raft with several other prospectors, and soon you're on your way.

By the time you reach the Klondike River, it's late autumn, and the days are getting shorter. You can see your breath in the morning. You hike several miles and find a not-too-crowded spot to set up your operation.

Men pan for gold in a narrow stream.

You begin panning for gold, but after a week, you've found little more than a few flakes. Should you be encouraged by those few flakes? Is there more in the area? Or should you move upriver a few miles?

- To stay here, turn to page 31.
- To move upriver, turn to page 32.

You take one last look over your shoulder at the many prospectors on the trail and decide to push onward. "Giddyup," you say.

Candy lumbers ahead obediently. At first, she handles the rocky passage well, but suddenly she twists her ankle and collapses. You managed to avoid injury in the fall, but Candy is badly hurt. Her leg is bent at a gross angle. You realize you have to put her down, and with a sad heart, you do. You understand now why the pass bears the nickname Dead Horse Trail.

Angry with yourself, you trudge onward. Now you're out of money, *and* you have no horse.

A few days later, you reach a gorge with a rushing river below. Mist from the crashing water floats in the air, and the sound is roaring. Someone has laid a long tree trunk across the gorge, and you decide to use it.

You cross safely with your first load of gear. Still feeling angry and wanting to hurry, you get a little careless as you're crossing back to get your next load. In one terrifying moment, you lose your balance and slip, hitting your head on the trunk before falling into the raging river below. You hit the rocks and feel a brief jolt of horrible pain. Then you feel nothing, as everything goes black.

THE END

To follow another path, turn to page 9.
To learn more about the Klondike Gold Rush, turn to page 101.

"Phillips," you say.

He drops what he was holding, but before he turns around, you fire. You can't take a chance that he might be armed too. Phillips falls over the side of the boat and dies.

"What is this?" someone yells.

Another prospector who's been camping just down the river enters your camp with his pistol drawn. Soon, two other prospectors also arrive.

"What happened here?" one of them asks.

"You killed him!" the first man says to you.

"He was stealing my gear," you insist.

"It's Phillips!" says the tallest man. "You shot Phillips!"

The first man goes to Phillips to check on him. "He's dead all right," he says softly.

The three men surround you. "He was stealing my gear," you say again.

"Phillips was not a thief," the tall one says. "He was my friend."

In a panic, you dart into the woods. You hear the men chasing after you. Then you hear a gunshot. A split second later, the bullet strikes you, and you fall forward from the impact. As you lay on the ground, facedown and bleeding, you realize you will die here, and you never even made it to the Klondike.

THE END

To follow another path, turn to page 9.
To learn more about the Klondike Gold Rush,
turn to page 101.

You cock your pistol. Phillips quickly drops what he was holding and stands, hands in the air.

"What are you doing?" you demand.

"I was checking out your boat," Phillips says. "You built a strong one."

"So what?" you say.

Phillips points to several packs of equipment on the ground. "I finally made enough money helping other men to buy my own gear," he says. "Now I want to find gold! Do you want a partner? You're good with wood. You built that boat—you can build a shelter on the river. I know the area better than anyone. We'll make a great team."

It might be a big help to have Phillips as a partner. Then again, you'll have to share whatever gold you find.

- To take him with you as a partner, turn to page 34.
- To go it alone, turn to page 37.

You've traveled a long time already and don't want to move again so soon. You decide to stick it out here.

Over the coming weeks, you find a few small stones and flakes of gold. It's not a lot—not even enough to pay your way back home—but you take it as a good sign. There must be more. Besides, you find that you enjoy this life—living off the land, panning for gold in the river, the excitement of possibly striking it rich at any moment.

You decide you like being a prospector. Whether you strike it rich or not, you may never go home.

THE END

To follow another path, turn to page 9.
To learn more about the Klondike Gold Rush, turn to page 101.

If there was a mother lode here, you would have found more by now. You decide to pack your gear and hike up the river. To your relief, the mosquitoes are dying out now, but the days are getting shorter and shorter. The nights are cold. At least you have warm clothes and a good tent.

You find a good spot and pitch camp. When you start panning again, you're rewarded with a handful of gold nuggets right away. You keep working and find more. You're starting to get excited when you hear a voice.

"Get out of here!" a man shouts. He has a long black beard and a rifle pointed at you. "You're on my claim!"

You don't believe him at first, but he has the paperwork. You are forced to move on—but not without giving up the gold you found. It's rightfully his.

Your spirit is crushed, but you vow to keep trying. You'll just have to be more careful about where you do your panning next time.

THE END

To follow another path, turn to page 9.
To learn more about the Klondike Gold Rush, turn to page 101.

You know Phillips is a hard worker, and after traveling up the White Pass Trail with him, you believe you can trust him. A partner would be nice to have in case you get hurt or need help hunting, prospecting, traveling, and so on.

"You've got a deal," you say.

The two of you shake on it. Early in the morning, you paddle the boat across the lake and onto the Yukon River. Together, you and Phillips begin the roughly 500-hundred mile journey to the Klondike.

On the third day, you hear rushing water up ahead.

"Rapids," Phillips says.

"Can we ride 'em?" you ask.

Phillips shakes his head. You have no choice but to beach the boat and continue on foot.

With Phillips's help, you carry your supplies over land until you're past the rapids. It takes several trips back and forth. The water crashes and foams on the rocks, and you realize it would have been impossible to paddle down.

A few days later, you reach the Klondike. Phillips suggests a spot that is several miles upriver. Helping all those prospectors, he learned a lot about where to find the best luck.

You set up camp on a wide bend where water runs clear. Then you begin to pan for gold. You dip your pan into the soil on the bottom of the river, pull it up, and shake it. You pick out the big rocks and toss them out into the water. You take more water into the pan and shake it some more.

As the sand and rock separate, you swirl it off the edges of the pan. Gold is much heavier than soil and rock, and it will lay in the bottom

Turn the page.

of the pan as you sift off the lighter materials. It simply takes patience.

Within an hour, a glint of something bright catches your eye in the pan. You dip in a bit more water and keep shaking off the rock and soil. And there it is—a big hunk of gold.

"I found some!" you call.

Phillips splashes through the water to your side. "By golly, you did!" he exclaims.

Over the next few weeks, you load your bags with gold. You've done what few others managed—struck it rich in the Klondike. You are only too happy to share the wealth with your partner and friend.

THE END

To follow another path, turn to page 9.
To learn more about the Klondike Gold Rush, turn to page 101.

"I don't think so," you say.

Phillips starts to argue, but when he sees the look in your eyes, he realizes that you've made up your mind.

"I'm sorry to hear that," he says.

The next day, you set out on your own. You get across the lake quickly, and to your delight, soon you're paddling up the Yukon River. You're making good time, but eventually you hear water rushing up ahead.

You realize there are probably some rapids. But they can't be bad, you reckon. After all, nobody warned you about them.

You continue on, and soon you've reached the start of the rapids. Unfortunately, they are violent and fast. You manage to steer your boat through the rocks for a while and are feeling proud, but then you smash into a rock just

Turn the page.

beneath the surface. The boat begins to flood with water.

You try to steer to the shore, but the boat is sinking too fast. You have to jump out. Your gear and the broken pieces of your boat bob and scatter in the rapids.

You fight your way through the rocks and rushing water. By the time you make it to shore, you're soaking wet, bruised, and cold. Your wrist feels broken. And now night is on you. You have nothing—no dry clothes, no tent, no food.

You're shivering, and then you see something that makes your heart sink further—snowflakes. You'll be lucky to survive three days out here alone.

THE END

To follow another path, turn to page 9.
To learn more about the Klondike Gold Rush,
turn to page 101.

CHAPTER 3

POLITICIAN

For the past four years you have served on the city council in Seattle, where you own a garment factory with your business partner, Magnussen. As you walk through the city, you see men begging in the street. Even people who have jobs are struggling to get by. Wages are down, and factories—like yours—are closing because there isn't enough business.

You've been lucky to stay afloat so far, but you worry about the future. Sales are already taking a dive, and you fear it's only going to get worse. That's one reason the idea of heading to the Klondike is so appealing.

Turn the page.

Another reason is the adventure. You've always dreamed of heading into the wilderness and living off the land. And with the possibility of riches beyond your wildest dreams, who wouldn't want to give it a shot?

In August, you and Magnussen agree to let your foreman run the factory and then buy tickets aboard a ship sailing out of Seattle. The wind rustles your hair, and you grin at Magnussen. You're actually doing it!

A steamer ship departs for the Yukon.

You sail up the Pacific, eventually landing in the town of St. Michael, Alaska, at the delta of the Yukon. It's autumn now, and the rivers will be icing over soon. You need to sail up the Yukon to the Klondike River while you still can.

You talk to a few folks down at the docks and meet the owners of a small private boat. One of them is a white man named James. His partner is a Koyukon man who goes by the nickname Hank.

"We have room for you and your partner," Hank says. He tells you their fee, and adds, "We're leaving first thing in the morning."

"There's a lot of gold just waiting to be plucked out of the ground," James adds, smiling.

You look at their boat. It's a flat-bottom raft that can fit the four of you and your gear. But if the rivers start icing over, you're not sure how

Turn the page.

well that boat will do. It's easy to imagine it getting crushed by floating ice floes.

On the other hand, Hank offers to help guide you if you come with them. For a fee, of course. It's not a bad idea.

"I don't know," Magnussen whispers to you. "Do you think we should trust these guys?"

James keeps smiling. "Well, there's a steamer heading out in five days. You could always join the dozens of other men who will be on that."

A big steamer does sound safer. But waiting five days and setting out with so many other prospectors isn't ideal.

• To go with Hank and James tomorrow, go to page 45.
• To wait and take the bigger boat, turn to page 47.

"I'm not waiting around to fight a hundred other guys for gold," you say to Magnussen. "Let's go with these two."

Magnussen agrees, and the next morning, you meet Hank and James at the dock bright and early. The four of you dip your paddles into the water, and you are off.

Turn the page.

Hank rigs up the sail, and the raft starts moving. Days go by, then weeks. You sail for hours while it's light and camp along the riverbanks at night. The water is cold, and you're glad you decided to go instead of waiting for the later boat.

Then one afternoon, you reach a narrow strait that has partly iced over.

"Go through," James says.

"No," Hank replies. "We have to go around. If it's part ice here, it'll be worse on the other end of the narrow where it tightens up."

"Go through," James insists. "We have axes and hammers. We can break up the ice. If we portage, we lose a week."

Hank turns to you. "You paid us," he says. "What do you want to do?"

- To press onward by water, turn to page 49.
- To portage, turn to page 52.

"I don't like the look of that little boat," Magnussen says. "I say we wait."

You're not totally convinced, but in the end you agree. Better to be safe than sorry. A few nights later, you're eating dinner in a tavern and fall into conversation with some men who are talking about the journey upriver. One of them, a prospector with a scar down his neck, says he's heard of several shipwrecks.

"My brother-in-law was on one of those ships," he adds. "If he's alive, he's stranded. Don't know if he's found food or shelter—or if he'll make it home."

"Winter's coming," says another prospector. "People are going to need help."

Later that night, in your bunkroom, Magnussen wakes you. "I was thinking . . ." he says.

Turn the page.

"Yeah?" you say.

"All those people out there. They need supplies. We could bring 'em. For a price."

You hesitate. It feels wrong to profit off someone else's misfortune. On the other hand, you know any of these men out here would do the same to you if they could. It wouldn't be too hard to buy some extra supplies now and sell them at a profit to anyone who needs them on the way.

- To buy extra food and supplies to sell at a profit, turn to page 53.
- To skip extra supplies, turn to page 56.

You've seen Hank and James navigate some tricky sections along the way so far. And you don't want to lose any time.

"You can handle this boat," you finally say. "Let's push through by water."

Hank shakes his head and looks down, but he agrees to give it a shot. You paddle into the strait, slowly and carefully. At first, the sheets of ice are only along the shore, making them easy to avoid.

But soon there are frozen shallow sections. At one point you reach an area with several large ice floes, and then you reach solid ice. You hack it with your axe over the front of the boat, and the other men paddle slowly into the openings you make.

Soon, it's too thick to break up from your position in the boat, and you gingerly step out onto the ice. It pops and cracks, but it holds you.

Turn the page.

You carry camping supplies to shore and start a fire. The four of you go to sleep that night without talking. You know you made the wrong choice.

In the morning, Hank says you need to pull the raft to shore. "Either that, or the shifting ice is going to chew it up," he says.

You don't argue. The four of you walk out onto the ice, chip the boat free from where it has frozen into the ice, and carry it ashore. It takes all day, so you camp another night.

The next day, you portage your supplies a few miles and get back into the river where the ice clears. But you only make it a couple miles before the ice closes off the river again. This time, you agree to get out and portage.

After this happens a third time, you realize you're not going to get any farther, so you pitch camp for the winter. Hank and James begin to cut timber to build a small cabin.

You and Magnussen go hunting. You don't find anything the first time out, and a small prick of panic pops up in the back of your mind. When the snow comes, you could be snowed in—no hunting at all, then. You better find meat and fast.

Either way, it's going to be a long winter with Hank and James. You'll be here for seven or eight months, you figure. You hope you can trust them because at this point, the idea of finding gold feels like a far-off fantasy.

THE END

To follow another path, turn to page 9.
To learn more about the Klondike Gold Rush,
turn to page 101.

You decide not to take any chances, so you beach the boat and carry it and your gear a couple of miles upriver. It's backbreaking work that takes more than a week. However when you reach the wider channel and load up the boat again, you feel good. You're safe, and you're sailing again.

For weeks you dodge ice floes and shifting sandbars. Hank and James are experts with their boat, and you come to trust them fully. When you finally arrive at the Klondike River, Hank reminds you of your discussion back in St. Michael.

"Stick with us, and we'll guide you," he offers.

You already paid them for passage on their boat. Guide services would be another fee, and if you found gold, you'd all share it. Or you and Magnussen could go on by yourselves.

• To stick with Hank and James, turn to page 58.
• To go it alone, turn to page 60.

You're out here to make money. Even if you don't find gold, you can make good money selling supplies. You decide to go for it.

You and Magnussen head to an outfitter in St. Michael and buy tents, blankets, boots, coats, tools, kerosene, and cured meat. You have a huge amount of gear, and the steamer captain charges you extra to store it all.

This is fine, but the first time you head below deck into the hold, you almost back out. It is dark and moldy. The hull itself is creaky and rotten. At this point you're committed, though, so you lash your gear together in the cleanest corner you can find and hope it will be okay.

Finally, the boat is chugging its way upriver. The river is quite icy, and the steamer moves slowly as the captain navigates the tricky channels to avoid the ice.

Turn the page.

You stand on the deck and watch nervously. A huge sheet of ice seems to be heading right for you, and the captain banks hard to avoid it. Suddenly, you feel scraping beneath your feet. The boat is dragging along the bottom. The captain tries to get it free, but finally he gives up.

"We're stuck!" someone yells.

"Let's get our stuff," you say to Magnussen.

You scramble below deck and begin unloading your gear. That's when you hear the sound of rushing water. There's a leak.

Some prospectors took the water route to the Yukon.

You move as fast as you can to get your gear out. It's dark when you are done. You stand on the shore and look at the boat listing sideways. The river is choked with ice, and the boat is useless. You're a long way from St. Michael and a long way from the Klondike—a long way from anywhere.

"We're here for the winter," Magnussen says.

You suppose he's right. Lucky for you, you bought all those extra supplies. It's going to be your fellow passengers who will end up buying it. You might make a decent profit off these people. You just hope you make it through the winter alive so you can enjoy it.

THE END

To follow another path, turn to page 9.
To learn more about the Klondike Gold Rush, turn to page 101.

You would rather focus on finding gold than making a little money off other prospectors, so you decide against purchasing any extra supplies.

Finally, the ship sets off for the Klondike. But it appears that winter is coming early—and with a fury. The river is icing over and snow is coming in on the wind. It stings when it hits your skin.

The captain pilots the boat skillfully, but his skill is no match for the weather. You're a couple hundred miles into your voyage when you get stuck in a shallow, icy strait. The wind gets worse, and the boat becomes encased in ice. The sails are pulled in, but the boat is already tipping sideways. Even with the sails in, the wind keeps pushing it over.

Some of the people onboard choose to abandon the ship and run across the icy river

to land. They look cold and wet out there. It might be safer in the boat. At least there you have shelter. That is, as long as it doesn't go under.

- To jump out and run across the ice to shore, turn to page 62.
- To stay with the boat where at least you're safe from the weather, turn to page 64.

"I like working with you men," you say to Hank. "Let's stick together."

Hank and James are happy to hear it. Together, the four of you continue up the river. Hank knows a good place to prospect, so you make camp at a wide bend in the river and build a wooden cabin that will stand up to the winter, which is rapidly coming. You begin panning for gold right away.

It turns out that Hank knew what he was talking about—you're pulling in pans full of gold before you know it. The four of your work hard

Prospectors panned for gold in rivers during the Gold Rush.

all day, but you can't help grinning at each other. You're going to be rich!

One afternoon, you and Magnussen come back from hunting a little early. As you approach camp, you overhear Hank and James whispering.

"Got to get the job done," Hank says.

You and Magnussen look at each other. What are Hank and James talking about? Are they planning to betray you and take the gold? Are they going to kill you? How well do you know these men, anyway?

"Let's confront them," Magnussen says. "Better to get it out in the open. At least we'll get a fair fight that way."

You're not so sure. It might be better not to let them know of your suspicions.

- To confront them about it, turn to page 66.
- To wait and see what happens, turn to page 68.

You and Magnussen talk it over. In the end, you figure the hardest part is behind you. You've read the papers—this river is loaded with gold. You don't need Hank and James's help, and you don't need to share your wealth with anyone.

"Thanks," you say to Hank. "You've been a big help, but we've got it from here."

You and Magnussen hike along the banks of the river for a week until you find a spot with a nice shallow bed for panning. It's also away from other prospectors.

The days are getting short, so you begin cutting timber for a cabin. But you spend plenty of time each day panning for gold. You find a few flakes, but nothing more.

You and Magnussen finish the cabin and settle in for the winter. You keep panning but never find anything substantial. By now, you

Prospectors stand near their winter lodging in Alaska.

realize you're stuck in this spot with no gold until spring. Not only that, but if you don't have better luck hunting, you will soon run out of food. The winter is going to be long, dark, and dangerous. You wonder how Hank and James are doing.

THE END

To follow another path, turn to page 9.
To learn more about the Klondike Gold Rush,
turn to page 101.

"I'm not going to stay in this lousy old boat and drown," you say to Magnussen. "Let's get our gear and go to shore."

He nods, and you grab as much of your gear as you can carry from the hold. Then you walk, slipping and falling, across the ice to the shore. A handful of other men do the same. The boat groans and tips, and you decide not to go back for the rest of your stuff.

You make a fire and camp for the night. In the morning, the ship is noticeably lower in the ice and water. The wind is still pummeling it. You're shivering and miserable, but it's clear the ship is going to sink.

"I say we go forward on foot," you say. "We can reach the Klondike in a couple weeks. Make shelter. Stick out the winter where the gold is."

Magnussen agrees, as do the others who followed you off the boat. The wind dies down, but unfortunately the snow starts falling even heavier. After a few days, it's up to your shins.

You keep going despite the sinking feeling in your stomach. You can't believe you never thought of it before—you might not live to see the spring.

THE END

To follow another path, turn to page 9.
To learn more about the Klondike Gold Rush, turn to page 101.

"I'm staying on board," Magnussen says. "At least we'll be out of the ice and wind."

You huddle beneath the deck and listen to the hull groaning and creaking in the wind. The next day, the wind gets even worse. You can hear sheets of wood tearing off the deck in the wind. Then the boat shifts, and suddenly water is gushing into the hold.

"Abandon ship!" the captain yells.

You and the rest of the passengers climb up to the deck, which is slick with ice and listing to the side. You slide down and crash through the railing onto the hard, icy surface of the river.

You regain your wits and stand up, but the ice is making crackling sounds. It's terrifying, and you make a dash for the shore.

Just as you do, the boat lurches and crashes through the ice, opening a huge hole. Water rushes across the ice, and soon you are caught up in it. The floe you're lying on tips upward, and you slide down it into the freezing water. Your last thought before you die is of the good life you had back in Seattle. You never should have left.

THE END

To follow another path, turn to page 9.
To learn more about the Klondike Gold Rush,
turn to page 101.

"Let's see what they have to say," you say.

You step into camp, and Magnussen says, "What are you talking about here all secret-like?"

"What are you planning?" you add.

"Planning?" Hank says. "Nothing."

But you see his hand reaching for the pistol on his belt. You draw first and shoot him. In the same moment, James fires his gun, and Magnussen drops. You shoot James.

You stand there amid the smell of gun smoke floating in the air. A moment ago, everything was fine. Now you're alone in the woods with three dead bodies. You begin to panic. But you realize what you have to do.

You spend the entire night digging three deep holes and burying the men. You spend the following weeks panning for gold, hunting, and staying warm in the cabin. The winter nights take up almost twenty-four hours of the day, and it's hard to keep your sanity. You need a good plan for the spring. You'll be carrying out a lot of gold—and you'll be down three men. What will you tell people? What if someone finds the bodies?

The good news is, you have many winter months to think about it.

THE END

To follow another path, turn to page 9.
To learn more about the Klondike Gold Rush, turn to page 101.

You decide to wait and see. Hank and James have been reliable partners so far. Maybe you're being paranoid.

That night, as you sit around the campfire eating dinner, everything seems normal again. Hank and James are joking around, and all four of you are talking about what you will do with your share of the money.

A few days pass, and you forget about your suspicions. You pass the long winter together. In the spring, the river thaws out and begins to run fast and hard. You load your supplies and gold onto the boat.

That's when Hank turns on you, his pistol in his hand.

"You can live or you can die," he says. "Either way, me and James will be leaving with this stuff, and you'll be staying here."

You reach for your own gun and point it at him, but when you pull the trigger, nothing happens. The chamber is empty.

"You took my bullets," you say.

James just grins.

You run at him, meaning to fight him, but Hank shoots you. Then he shoots Magnussen.

"I guess you choose die," he says.

THE END

To follow another path, turn to page 9.
To learn more about the Klondike Gold Rush, turn to page 101.

CHAPTER 4

NEW YORK TEAM

You own a gymnasium in New York City, where you live with your wife and two children. You have a good life, but when news of the Klondike gold rush reaches New York, something changes inside you. The idea of going on a grand adventure—and coming home rich—is thrilling.

When you mention the idea to your wife, she tells you it's a terrible idea. "Don't go," she says. "What would the kids and I do if something happened to you?"

Turn the page.

You have to admit, it is a dangerous trip. You've read the stories of people freezing to death, getting trapped in avalanches, and simply disappearing. To give yourself a better chance, you decide to put together a large team. You put an ad in a local paper, and the response is strong. Soon you've assembled a group of 18 men, including a doctor, a mineralogist, a pastor, a couple of police officers, and more. Two of the men are experienced orienteers. Since you're the one paying them, you are the boss of the team.

You and the team take the train across the country to Seattle, where you buy all the supplies you'll need, including dogs and sleds. You even buy a large dynamo engine to power your camp once you establish it. When you find the cost of boat tickets to be outrageous, you find a battered old ship for sale and buy that. You fix it up, hire a captain, and set off for Alaska.

Most men who take the water route to the Klondike sail all the way up to St. Michael, Alaska, and then up the Yukon River. But you have a different plan. You sail to the southern part of the Alaskan peninsula with the plan of hiking over the glacier and the mountain beyond it, right onto the Yukon River. The journey should be shorter than sailing to St. Michael, and you'll avoid the crime-ridden boomtowns and the long, perilous river trip from the coast.

You're feeling smug about your plan until you approach the Alaskan coast and look up at the towering glacier. It is terrifyingly huge. Your heart hammers in your chest with fear and excitement.

You hit shore in mid-April and unload the boat, making camp for the night before crossing the vast field of snow and ice on the way to the glacier. After a week, you reach it and begin climbing. You are trudging along when suddenly

Turn the page.

you hear a slippery sound like sheets being pulled across a bed. That noise is followed by a grunt and a scream.

You look up. The doctor who was walking ahead of you has disappeared. You freeze in your tracks, and everyone behind you stops. Peering ahead, you can see an open crevasse in the ice that had been hidden by snow. You lean over, but it's dark and deep. You can't see the bottom.

"Help!" the doctor cries out. "Please!" His voice sounds very far away.

One of the orienteers comes to your side. "We'll never be able to reach him," he says. "We could lose more men if we try."

You see his point, but it seems cruel to just leave the doctor to die.

- To lower a man down on a rope to try to rescue him, go to page 75.
- To leave him behind, turn to page 78.

"We can't just let him die," you say. "It may be dangerous, but we have to try to rescue him."

One of the police officers volunteers to go down. You tie a rope around his waist, and three of the men hold onto the other end as he rappels down. Everyone stays away from the lip of the opening, hoping that snow doesn't avalanche into it.

The men let out more than 500 feet of rope before it stops. Several minutes later, the police officer gives a tug, and the men pull him out.

Turn the page.

Amazingly, he emerges with the doctor tied to his back. He is cold and wet but unhurt. The fall was softened by the snow.

The group carefully navigates around the opening and continues its journey up the glacier. Several days later, as you are setting up camp near the top of the glacier, you realize someone is missing—Headrick, the team member who was taking up the rear of the line. He was working with the sled dogs to drag the engine.

"Where's Headrick?" you ask aloud.

Nobody has seen him, so you send the two police officers—Sullivan and Rogers—back to look for him. But two hours later, only Sullivan returns.

"Found Headrick," he says. "He's dead—fell off a ridge. Must've dropped hundreds of feet onto the ice."

"Where's Rogers?" you ask.

"He slipped off and died too," the man says. Tears form in his eyes and freeze to his face.

The camp is silent and sullen that night. Your party of 18 is now 16. The next day, however, there is no choice but to go on. You have to go down the other side of the glacier and cross a dangerous field of ridges and crevasses to reach the mountain. Sullivan suggests that you abandon the engine.

"It's too risky to carry over the open ice," he says. "It's heavy and hard to maneuver."

You don't strictly *need* the engine. But you know it's going to make your camp a lot warmer and more efficient if you have it. Plus, you spent a great deal of money on the thing.

- To abandon the engine, turn to page 81.
- To keep the engine, turn to page 83.

It's too risky to send another man into the dangerous crevasse.

"Let's move on," you say.

Some of the men gape at you as if they can't believe it. "You're just going to let him die down there?" one of the orienteers asks.

"Listen," you say, pointing to the opening. No sounds reach your ears. "He's not yelling anymore. He's probably dead already. It's a terrible thing, but it's the smart thing. We have to move on."

You continue hiking for several more days. Several of the men are losing their eyesight because of the relentless glare off the ice and snow. You all wear dark goggles, but they barely help. Eventually you all cover your goggles with a bandana and look straight down as you walk. It's risky because you could hit another crevasse, but it's better than burning your eyes and going blind.

Finally, you crest the glacier. The hike down the other side is still dangerous, but at least it's easier. You make it to the bottom safely before facing another challenge. The floating glacier crashes against the rocks at the base of the mountain, crushing and grinding rocks and ice.

Turn the page.

You can see trees on the mountain high above, and you thrill at the idea of having actual earth beneath your feet. But first you must cross this maze of ice bridges and drop-offs. You can hear water rushing invisibly somewhere beneath your feet.

It must be nearly ten o'clock at night, but the sun won't set for a few more hours. Some of the men are eager to get across and camp on solid ground tonight. You can gather wood, build a fire, dry your clothes, and cook meat.

On the other hand, you've been hiking for more than 12 hours. You all could use the rest. It would be safer to camp here and go in the morning.

- To camp tonight and rest up, turn to page 85.
- To cross now, turn to page 87.

You hate to do it, but you agree that the engine makes your trip too dangerous.

"Leave it here," you say.

The men unstrap it from the sled. As an added bonus, this means the dogs can pull some of the other supplies, reducing what everyone has to carry.

With the lighter load, you make it quickly and safely across the ice to the solid ground.

A Klondike dog team

Turn the page.

It's summer now, and snow is melting rapidly, rushing down the mountain in swift lines. One day you see a moose and shoot it, and that night you build a big campfire and grill the meat. The men are happy, chattering excitedly as they eat. Even the dogs seem to be in a good mood as they chew on the bones.

A few days later you reach a creek. It's not the Yukon, but some of the men are eager to begin panning for gold.

"This is what we came for," Sullivan says. "Let's take a few days and see what we find." Several men nod in agreement.

It's still a couple hundred miles to the Klondike, the only place you *know* there is gold. Panning here is likely just a waste of time. On the other hand, you want to keep the team happy.

- To start panning for gold now, turn to page 89.
- To push onto the Klondike, turn to page 92.

The engine is too important to abandon. You've invested money and time into getting it here. You're not going to give it up now. So you begin the slow journey across to the solid ground.

You move carefully, maneuvering around smaller crevasses. When you come to an opening too big to skirt, you use ropes to rappel down to the bottom. You lower the gear, including the engine, and haul it across the cold, dark bottom of the icy canyon.

Turn the page.

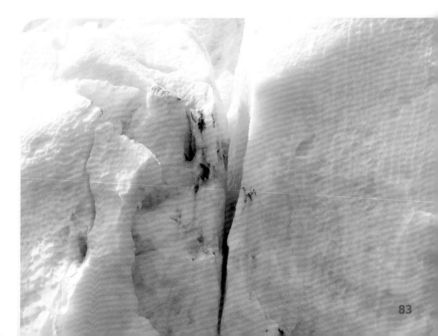

You're leading the way and are almost to the other side of the crevasse when you hear a crack echo through the canyon. Your first thought is that someone fired their gun. But then you hear another crack, then another, and then a long, creaking sound.

The ground shifts beneath your feet and suddenly disappears. You plunge through darkness into icy cold water. The gear on your back pulls you down deeper. Your last thought before you die is to hope that the other men make it.

THE END

To follow another path, turn to page 9.
To learn more about the Klondike Gold Rush,
turn to page 101.

You decide to camp. Some of the men complain, but in the morning, everyone's spirits are high. The rest did you good, and you cross the dangerous field of icy crevasses in a day. The earth feels solid beneath your feet. You and the men grin at one another. It feels like the journey is only going to get easier from here.

You start up the mountain. Away from the ice, your snow blindness begins to fade. Days go by, then weeks. The summer blossoms hot and buggy. Bumblebees the size of your thumb buzz through fields of wildflowers.

Unfortunately, the mosquitoes swarm you day and night, and you scratch your bites constantly. One morning, you find it hard to get out of bed. You feel hot and exhausted. You have a fever.

One of the men, Sullivan, checks on you and just shakes his head. You know you must look bad.

Turn the page.

"Let's camp a couple days and let the boss heal," he announces to the rest of the group.

Unfortunately, your fever only gets worse. A couple of the other men in camp get fevers too. You see a vision of the doctor you left in the crevasse to die. He is looking at you sadly. You realize you're hallucinating. You realize you never should have left him behind. He had all the medicine and medical gear with him. His anguished, dying cries mix with your own as you close your eyes for the last time.

THE END

To follow another path, turn to page 9.
To learn more about the Klondike Gold Rush,
turn to page 101.

The temptation to camp on solid ground is too strong.

"Gear up, men," you say. "We're crossing tonight."

You set off, and at first everything is fine. You skirt some tricky openings and avoid a loose ice floe. But then one of the men—a police officer named Rogers—slips and falls. Just as he's about to get back up, he begins to slide away from the group. You realize he's on a slope. Soon Rogers simply slips off the horizon and disappears. An hour later, you lose another man.

Finally, you reach the solid ground. The camp is quiet that night as everyone thinks about the two lost men.

The following week, as you're hiking over the mountain, two men come down with bad fevers. They can't go on, so you decide to camp for a

Turn the page.

few nights and see if they recover. Without the doctor and the medicine he was carrying, there isn't much else you can do.

After two nights, the men are even worse. You wait another couple of days, and finally they die.

Headrick, the man in charge of the dogs, is the first one to suggest going home. "It's not worth it," he says. "We're losing men fast. Any one of us could be next."

Another man agrees. "We're not far from Dawson City, the boomtown on the Yukon," he says. "We could book passage home on a ship."

• To push onward, turn to page 94.
• To relent and go home, turn to page 96.

You decide to camp and see if you find any gold. You could all use a rest anyway.

At first, it seems to pay off. One of the men finds some gold stones on the second day. But when Jim Brown, the mineralogist, examines the stones, he shakes his head.

"Fool's gold," Brown says. It's what people call pyrite, a mineral that looks like gold but is worthless.

You move up the creek and keep working, and you find enough gold to keep the men excited. It's still warm now, but the days are quickly getting shorter. You know it will be winter soon enough.

Finally you press on, but you've lost weeks of precious warm weather. Snow begins to fall, and by the time you reach the Yukon, you have to stop and build a cabin for winter. The Klondike will have to wait until spring.

Turn the page.

You get the cabin built and manage to shoot some elk for meat. Weeks pass, then months. Before long, food is running low, and so are everyone's spirits. The cabin is small and cold. Men argue about stupid things. Everyone is thin and weak.

One dark day, when you are chopping wood for the fire, you accidentally break the head of Sullivan's axe.

"You idiot!" he says and reaches for his pistol.

"Whoa!" you say. "I'll replace the axe."

You manage to calm him down, but you realize everyone is losing their grip on sanity. Then one morning you wake up groggy and weak to see three of the men standing by the door.

"We're going home," Sullivan says. "We can't take this anymore."

The other men look at them. You can tell they are considering joining them. You're so weak and hungry, it's hard to think straight. Maybe you should join them too.

• To go with them, turn to page 98.
• To stay here, turn to page 99.

"Let's not be fools!" you yell. "We know where the gold is, and it's not here. We must continue!"

Some of the men nod in agreement, though you can tell others are angry. Still, the team continues. You move quickly and carefully and reach the Klondike River just as winter arrives.

As snow falls, the river begins to ice over. You build a cabin with a fireplace made from river stones. You hunt and fish and cut down trees, stockpiling food and wood for the winter. Even with all these precautions, the winter is very difficult. In a few months, your food stores are almost gone, and everyone is extremely hungry.

Finally, after months of darkness and bitter cold, you see something beautiful—a streak of light on the horizon. It's the first sign of daylight in months. Winter is ending. You still have a long way to go, but this sight gives all of you hope and renewed strength.

Soon, the snow and ice are melting. Camp is muddy and sloppy, but you're all focused on the task at hand. You cut down more trees and build a shaker box. You pour sand, rocks, and water from the river into it and shake it so the rocks, dirt, and water flow off the end, leaving anything heavier—such as gold—behind.

The camp is alive with activity. Men are panning for gold with pans. Others are loading the shaker box. Still others are hunting, fishing, cooking, and mending clothes. It's not long before gold shows up in the shaker box. The men using pans are finding gold too. You realize you've chosen the perfect spot. There's enough gold here to make all of you filthy rich!

THE END

To follow another path, turn to page 9.
To learn more about the Klondike Gold Rush,
turn to page 101.

"We are not turning back now!" you yell. "We're so close. We continue on."

You're the boss and should get to make the call. The men, however, don't seem to respect your authority anymore. Most of them gather their gear and leave.

Once they've gone, it's only you, your friend Ferguson, and the mineralogist Jim Brown left in camp. It's obvious you have to abandon the engine, so you continue your journey without it. It's difficult going, and thoughts of the dead men haunt you. Only your dreams of gold keep you going.

You make slow progress with the smaller team, and winter returns before you reach the Yukon. Due to your exhaustion and desperation to make progress, you grow careless about where you hike and camp.

One morning you wake up in your tent to a rumbling sound outside. You step outside and look around. You're camped in a valley, which protected you from the wind, but now the air is clouded with wind and snow. And the rumbling is getting louder.

You glance up and see a massive wall of snow tumbling down the slope toward you. You wonder if the avalanche will crush you instantly or if you'll suffocate to death. Either way, your dreams of striking it rich will die with you.

THE END

To follow another path, turn to page 9.
To learn more about the Klondike Gold Rush, turn to page 101.

You realize the team is united against you. Your poor decisions have caused them to lose faith, and now you have a mutiny on your hands.

"Fine," you say.

You change course and head toward Dawson City. The men were right—it was not too far. When you arrive, you find the boomtown to be busy and exciting. You eat the best dinner of your entire life in a tavern. You haven't had good cooked meat in so long.

Dawson City was a booming town during the Gold Rush.

When you ask the tavern owner about it, he admits that it's horse meat. Many horses die on this journey, and this is how he makes his business. You don't care—it was exactly what you needed.

You talk with some of the other travelers in the tavern about your adventure. Some of them have failed and returned, and they nod along with your story. They understand.

Others—men who recently arrived in Dawson City on steamer ships or from the overland route—listen carefully, but they're not deterred. They still plan to go out in search of their fortune. You wish them luck. As for you and your men, you just want to go home.

THE END

To follow another path, turn to page 9.
To learn more about the Klondike Gold Rush, turn to page 101.

"Yes," you say weakly. "You're right. Let's get out of here."

You step out into cold night and begin pushing your way through the chest-high snow. It doesn't take long before you are trembling with cold. Have you even made it a hundred yards? You have no idea.

Soon, the snow is higher than your head. You remember reading that the temperature here this time of year is at least 50 degrees below zero. You can't feel any part of your body. You suddenly realize you can't see, either. Everything is black. Where are the other men? You can't see them or hear them. You slump forward, but the snow holds your body mostly upright. You fall into a deep, deathly sleep.

THE END

To follow another path, turn to page 9.
To learn more about the Klondike Gold Rush, turn to page 101.

Your head is foggy, but you know that trying to leave in the middle of winter without supplies is not a smart idea.

"Don't go," you say. "You must not go."

Brown sides with you. "We will find gold," the mineralogist says. "We're close."

Six of the men leave anyway. Besides Brown, the police officer and one of your good friends from home have stayed behind. The doctor is with you as well. These men are brave and strong. And Brown's words give you hope. This is a good core team. You will find gold in the spring. You know it. You will return home to your wife and children next year, rich beyond your wildest dreams. You believe it. You have no other choice.

THE END

To follow another path, turn to page 9.
To learn more about the Klondike Gold Rush,
turn to page 101.

CHAPTER 5

GOLD IN THE KLONDIKE!

In August 1896, a man named Jim "Skookum" Mason and his family discovered gold in a creek near the Klondike River in the Yukon Territory of Canada. As news of the discovery spread, prospectors in the area swarmed the Klondike and began staking claims. It quickly became apparent that there was gold in the area—and lots of it.

It took months for the news to reach the rest of the world. When it did, people from all over started stampede to the Klondike. Prospectors could choose one of several routes, but the options fell into three main categories. Most chose the overland route, which was the least expensive. They sailed from Seattle to one of two towns on the Gulf of Alaska—Skagway or Dyea. These tiny tent communities turned into burgeoning boomtowns in a matter of months.

From there, prospectors made their way up the White Pass Trail from Skagway or the Chilkoot Trail from Dyea to cross the Coast Range Mountains. Pack animals, such as horses and mules, often dropped dead from exhaustion on the White Pass Trail. Others injured themselves on the rocky terrain and had to be put down. Without the help of animals, prospectors were forced to haul their gear in stages. On the other side of the mountains, they reached the head of the Yukon River, where they would travel by handmade boat about 500 miles to the Klondike River.

Men, hoping to strike it rich, streamed into the Klondike during the Gold Rush.

Those who could afford to do so chose the all-water route. They sailed from San Francisco or Seattle to St. Michael, on the northern side of Alaska, and then down the Yukon River to the boomtown of Dawson City. There, they accessed the Klondike River. This route was faster and safer than the overland route, but as demand increased, so did the price of boat tickets. Nearly 2,000 stampeders attempted this route in 1897. Nearly all of them got stuck when the river iced over in October.

Still others chose the "all-Canada route." They traveled by land from Edmonton, Canada, to Dawson City. This route was more popular with Canadian and British stampeders. The trails were primitive and often nonexistent. Getting across the swamps, slush, ice, and mud was exhausting and could be deadly to humans and pack animals alike.

It's estimated that between 1896 and 1899, about 100,000 stampeders attempted to reach the Klondike and strike it rich. Of those, between 30,000 and 40,000 made it to Dawson City. Fewer than that actually got onto the Klondike. Those who did panned for gold in the river and dug mine shafts into the earth. Fewer than 4,000 people found gold there, and of them, only a few hundred actually became rich.

There were many reasons for this. For one, local prospectors had snatched up most of the worthwhile claims by the time most stampeders arrived. Stampeders also faced many dangers and challenges along their journey. The boomtowns were rife with crime and inflated prices. Out on the trails and rivers, there was little in the way of law, and men were sometimes murdered or robbed. The work of hauling gear in stages was backbreaking, and many gave up. Men faced starvation, hypothermia, avalanche, and disease. They could be injured, get lost, or get stranded. Many died. Most went home broke.

Over time, Dawson City—the wild boomtown that connected most of the world to the Klondike—grew into a more sophisticated tourist town. That made it less appealing to

Dawson City in the late 1890s

adventure seekers. Telegraph and train lines eventually reached the area as well. In time, with so few people actually striking it rich, the excitement of the Klondike died down. When gold was discovered elsewhere in Canada and Alaska, the world's attention shifted to those locales. By 1899, the Klondike gold rush was finished.

Klondike Gold Rush Timeline

1895–1896: Gold reserves in the United States drop, causing an economic depression; banks close, while poverty and unemployment soar.

August 16, 1896: A group of prospectors, including Skookum Jim, discover gold on Bonanza Creek, a tributary of the Klondike River in Yukon Territory.

August 1896: Local prospectors claim all claims on Rabbit Creek, a tributary of the Klondike River.

Fall of 1896: More gold is found in Klondike tributaries; as news begins to spread, area miners begin traveling toward the Klondike.

January 1897: A small settlement at the junction of the Klondike and Yukon Rivers is named Dawson City as its population swells to 500 people.

June 1897: Boats loaded with gold begin departing the Yukon.

July 14, 1897: The first prospectors, carrying huge amounts of gold and news of more to be found, reach San Francisco, California.

July 19, 1897: The first ship leaves the U.S. for the Klondike.

Summer of 1897: Tens of thousands of people, all hoping to find gold, head for the Klondike.

Spring 1898: The population of Dawson City and its surrounding area reaches 30,000 people.

Summer of 1898: Stampeders—discouraged at not finding gold and finding it difficult to make a living—begin leaving the Klondike.

September 22, 1898: Gold is discovered in Nome, Alaska.

August 1899: Prospectors leave Dawson City by the thousands and head for Nome, signaling the end of the Klondike Gold Rush.

Other Paths to Explore

1. Those who decided to seek gold in the Klondike knew it would be a very difficult journey, yet they did it anyway. What factors would go into this decision for you? What would it take for you to decide to go for it?

2. Imagine you found a huge amount of gold in the Klondike region. What would you do with your riches?

3. Most people who went to the Klondike in search of gold failed to find any. If they didn't die on the way, they returned home broke. What would that feel like? Do you think it would have been worth the adventure, even though you came home with nothing? Why or why not?

Select Bibliography

Berton, Pierre. *Klondike Fever: The Life and Death of the Last Great Gold Rush.* New York: Basic Books, 1959.

Castner, Brian. *Stampede: Gold Fever and Disaster in the Klondike.* New York: Double Day, 2021.

History.com: Klondike Gold Rush
www.history.com/topics/19th-century/klondike-gold-rush

Read More

Doeden, Matt. *Can You Survive Hair-Raising Mountain Encounters?: An Interactive Wilderness Adventure.* North Mankato, MN: Capstone Press, 2023.

Lourie, Peter. *Jack London and the Klondike Gold Rush.* New York: Henry Holt and Co., 2017.

Meissner, David, and Kim Richardson. *Call of the Klondike: A True Gold Rush Adventure.* Honesdale, PA: Calkins Creek, 2019.

Internet Sites

Alaska Kids: Gold Rush
www.alaskakids.org/index.cfm/know-alaska/Alaska-History/Gold-Rushes

Britannica Kids: Gold Rush
kids.britannica.com/students/article/gold-rush/274596

Kiddle: Klondike Gold Rush Facts for Kids
kids.kiddle.co/Klondike_Gold_Rush

National Park Service: Klondike Gold Rush: What Was the Klondike Gold Rush?
www.nps.gov/klgo/learn/goldrush.htm

Glossary

avalanche (A-vuh-lanch)—a large mass of ice, snow, or earth that suddenly moves down the side of a mountain

boomtown (BOOM-town)—a town experiencing a sudden growth in business and population, usually because something valuable, such as gold, has been discovered nearby

crevasse (kri-VAS)—a deep, wide crack in a glacier or sheet of ice

delta (DEL-tuh)—the triangle-shaped area where a river deposits mud, sand, and pebbles

foreman (FOHR-muhn)—a person in charge of a group of workers, especially in a factory

glacier (GLAY-shur)—a huge moving body of ice found in mountain valleys or polar regions

gorge (GORJ)—a canyon with steep walls that rise straight upward

hypothermia (hyp-poh-THUR-mee-uh)—a life-threatening condition that occurs when a person's body temperature falls several degrees below normal

ice floe (AHYS FLOH)—a large, flat sheet of floating ice

kerosene (KER-uh-seen)—a thin, colorless fuel that is made from petroleum

livery stable (LIH-vuh-ree STAY-buhl)—a stable where horses and vehicles are kept for hire and where horses may be stabled

mineralogist (mih-nuh-RAH-luh-jist)—a scientist who studies minerals

mutiny (MYOO-tuh-nee)—a revolt or rebellion against the person in charge

orienteer (or-ee-uhn-TIHR)—a person who finds their way across rough, unfamiliar land using a map and compass

paranoid (PAR-uh-noyd)—extremely fearful

portage (POOR-tij)—the carrying of boats or goods overland from one body of water to another

prospector (PRAA-spek-tur)—a person who looks for valuable minerals, especially silver and gold

recession (ri-SEH-shuhn)—a temporary slowing of business activity

satchel (SAH-chuhl)—a small bag, often with a shoulder strap

strait (STRAYT)—a narrow waterway connecting two large bodies of water

tributary (TRIH-byuh-ter-ee)—a stream or river that flows into a larger stream or river

JOIN OTHER HISTORICAL ADVENTURES WITH MORE
YOU CHOOSE SEEKING HISTORY!

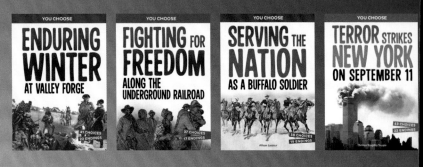

About the Author

Eric Braun is the author of dozens of books for young readers on topics ranging from sports and history to fractured fairy tales and middle grade fiction. Besides stories, he loves bike riding, camping, adventures, and wearing hats. Learn more at heyericbraun.com.